ON THE SHOULDERS OF
GIANTS
ANGELS

By Dr. Delece Williams

Instead Of Straddling The Fence,

Become The Fence

Volume 3—All Inspirational

(Including Self-Reflection Workbook Pages)

AuthorHouse™
1663 Liberty Drive
Bloomington, IN 47403
www.authorhouse.com
Phone: 833-262-8899

Because of the dynamic nature of the Internet, any web addresses or links contained in this book may have changed
since publication and may no longer be valid. The views expressed in this work are solely those of the author and do not
necessarily reflect the views of the publisher, and the publisher hereby disclaims any responsibility for them.

Any people depicted in stock imagery provided by Getty Images are models,
and such images are being used for illustrative purposes only.
Certain stock imagery © Getty Images.

Scripture quotations marked KJV are from the Holy Bible, King James Version (Authorized Version). First published
in 1611. Quoted from the KJV Classic Reference Bible, Copyright © 1983 by The Zondervan Corporation.

This book is printed on acid-free paper.

ISBN: 979-8-8230-4669-5 (sc)
ISBN: 979-8-8230-4670-1 (e)

Print information available on the last page.

Published by AuthorHouse 04/10/2025

authorHOUSE®

THE AUTHOR'S GOAL
COMMUNICATION IS EVERYTHING

It's the exchange of ideas and information by talk, prayer, gesture, or writing. It is an active process, present in all meaningful relationships. Communication is not only talking, but also listening, looking and feeling. Though individuals have different communication styles, spiritually mature people (believers in Christ) are to seek continually to improve their communication with other people and with God through prayer, action and obedience.

What we say is powerful. The spoken word can either speak life, encourage or discourage. Scripture teaches believers to control the tongue (James 3:1-12) and speak only words of kindness, even in correction (Eph. 4:29, 32). The Book of Proverbs also discusses the importance of listening with understanding from others who speak.

Communication is more than conveying information, it also gives advice about verbal behavior and spiritual guidance. Christians are to: *speak the truth in love *control angry words *speak words of exaltation, encouragement and healing *avoid unkind or bitter words *speak words of forgiveness.

Mature believers realize that clear, loving communication is important in conveying the message of salvation.

Some of this passage of understanding in expression of communication comes from the Women's Study Bible.

Dr.Delece.com

THIS BOOK BELONGS TO:
_____

The 3D Affect
(Dr. Delece's Destiny Affecting Others)
God Bless

OTHER BOOKS

"ON THE SHOULDERS OF GIANTS"
Volume 1 - Lessons & Blessings
Volume 2 -Youth Edition

GO TO:

www.drdelece.com
drdelece@hotmail.com

PREFACE

Have you ever heard of the saying, "**STANDING IN SOMEONE ELSE'S SHOES**," as a point of reference to learning a lesson? Well, what happens when the shoes doesn't fit? In this book, we'll show you how to **"STAND ON THE SHOULDERS OF ANGELS"** as a stepping stone through the unction of **God's Holy Spirit** (*his power*) for victorious living. As we gras guidance, leadership and correction of **God's word** *(the bible),* we are destined to grow according to his will for prosperity and more, thus denouncing sin, shame and defeat.

The author, **Dr. Delece** talks about her experiences of learning to lean on her faith in God while using stirring words by way of **quotes from some famous individuals and powerful biblical scriptures** to help prepare you for better understanding, awareness and growth.

TEACHABLE MOMENTS, DISCLOSURE Each page highlights a teachable moment from a short quote spoken by well-known figures from ancient times to present day, and some **wisdom points from the Bible** to show how throughout history people agreed about certain basic approaches to life for victories in different ways according to their faith.

One of the World's Greatest Gospel Voices, Yolanda Adams and I *(One of my favorite Inspirations).*

Delece was becoming famous according to the world, but...

Each quote is taken from the **Book of Positive Quotations, Compiled and Arranged by John Cook** and **Bible scriptures or a message taken from the New Kings James Version, Women's Study guide.**

The subtitle of this book, "*Instead of Straddling the Fence, Be the Fence,*" is themed and referenced from a bible scripture (**Do not straddle the Fence - 1 Corinthians 10:12-22**). *It relates to how we should not be in love with the worldly ways of living, once we choose to live for God. We have to make a dedicated stand to live according to Godly principles.*

It is Dr. Delece's goal to convey thought provoking wisdom regarding one major struggle that a person may have, who once lived for the excitement of the world and is now living for God's purpose. Towards the back of the book, there are **Self-Reflection Workbook pages for questions concerning your spiritual inquisitiveness.** The Bible, tells us to not love the things in this world *(1 John 2:15-17)* so, what should you do while trying to fit in this world with religion? Let's learn some wisdom points from our Gospel giants as we stand on their shoulders together.

Dedication

I would like to dedicate every word to the millennials, working professionals, single parents and others who need inspiration in discovering their greatest potential for living their best life.

Dear God, thank you for bringing out the best in me. Farley Keith Williams (Husband), thanks for being my best friend. To my daughter, Danielle McDuffy (Dejhan) Means, grand children, Dior, Dion & Dejhan Jr, thank you. To my siblings, sisters, Andrena (Keith) Griffin, Yaminah (Malcolm) Mason, Jerelene (Sidney) Jackson and brothers, Victor McDuffy and Leonard (Kentrice) Hannah and step children, Jasmin and Keith, we grew together.

To the Kidz Korna team, from our grass-root youth organization, thank you for helping to shape the lives of many young people for over 30 years. Thank you parents for allowing your kids to be apart of our experience of which was my inspiration to write this book.

Thank You Jesus!

Copyright@ 2012 by
drdelece@hotmail.com
www.drdelece.com

ANGELS ON THE SHOULDERS OF GIANTS

Volume 3– All Inspirational including Workbook Pages

Celebrities with Delece

*Keanu Reeves

Yolanda Adams

*Tyler Perry

*Iyanla Vanzant

*Tye Tribbet

Grant Hill

*Katherine Jackson

Table of Content

1. GOD LOVES US (John 3:16) , Quote By *David Jenkins*..Page 06
2. WHO AM I, WHO IS GOD (Psalms 36:5), Quote By *Max Lerner*..Page 07
3. WHAT IS PRAYER (James 5:16), Quote By *Samuel M. Shoemaker*..Page 08
4. FAITH AND WORKS (James 2:14), Quote By *John Jay Chapman* ..Page 09
5. KEYS TO SPIRITUAL SUCCESS (1 Peter 3:3-4), Quote By *Thomas B. Brooks*..Page 10
6. WHAT DOES SALVATION MEAN (Romans 10:9), Quote By *John Laidlaw*..Pg. 11
7. PRAISE AND WORSHIP, (Psalms 22:3), Quote By *Charles Haddon Spurgeon*..Page 12
8. CHURCH, SPIRITUAL AWARENESS (Ephesians 6:12), Quote By *Carlo Carretto*..Pg.13
9. WORSHIP & FASTING (Matthews 6: 16-18), Quote By *Vance Harner*.. Page 14
10. THE BIBLE, FORGIVENESS (Matthew 17:21), Quote By *Abraham Lincoln*...Page 15
11. GOD'S GUIDANCE, Quote By *The work of the Chariot*...Page 16
12. THE FOOLISH THINGS (1Corinthians 1:27), Quote By *Shakiti Gawain*..Page 17
13. ANGELS ARE REAL, Quote By *Henry Sloane Coffin*...Page 18
14. GOD'S FAVOR, GRACE AND MERCY (Psalms 37:4), Quote By *Emmanuel*...Page 19
15. MY MANY BLESSINGS , Quote By *Martin Luther*....Page 20
16. STRADDLING THE FENCE (Romans 8:35-39), Quote By *Joseph Addition*..Page 21
17. TAKE THIS WITH YOU, IN CASE YOU NEED (Multiple Scriptures) ....Page 22

18. SELF REFLECTION WORK BOOK PAGES.....Pages 23 – 41
    *Putting God First (Exodus 20:3) -Page 24
    *Attitude-(Philippians 2:5) -Page 25
    *Asking God For Help (Mathew 7:7-8) -Pg 26
    *Anxiety (1 Peter 5:7) -Page 27
    *God Guidance (Proverbs 3:5-6) -Page 28
    *Gratitude (Proverbs 10:6) -Page 29
    *Listening to God (Isaiah 55:3)) -Page 30
    *Patience (Proverbs 19:11) -Page 31
    *Dealing with Change (Ecclesiastes 3:1)-Pg 32
    *Priorities-(Mathew 6:33) -Page 33
    *Perseverance (Galatians 6:9) -Page 34
    *Procrastination (James 1:22) -Page 3!
    *Understanding (Psalms 119:33) -Page 36
    *Responsibility (Galatians 6, 4;5)-Pg 37
    *Spiritual Growth (2 Timothy 1:6) -Page 38
    *Prayer (Philippians 4:6) -Page 39
    *Negativity (Psalm 118-5) -Page 40
    *Self-Examination (Mathew 7:3-5)-Pg 41

19. Join Us!....Our Daily Prayerline Information...Page 42

20. BEFORE YOU CLOSE THIS BOOK......Page 43

21. GOING BACK TO GO FORWARD BY DR. DELECE.....Pages 44 & 45

22. Close Out Quote By **Benjiman Franklin** ...Page 46

23. Other Books Available...Page 47

GOD LOVES US

One of my headshots

Like any professional job interview, you must have some credentials in order to get the job. This book is filled with some of my professional acting and modeling photos which were some of my credentials in order to succeed in show business. This journey also caused me to get close to GOD. Join me as I take you on my spiritual awakening experiences during my quest for success in show business from Hollywood to New York and lots more.

I remember being a kid who did not grow up in Church, but I was always told that **God loves me and Jesus does too**. Here's a scripture from the Bible to back it up. **(John 3:16 — *For God so loved the World, that he gave his only begotten son*)**.

> **No statement about God is simply, literally true. God is far more than can be measured, described, defined in ordinary language, or pinned down to any particular happening.**
> **By David Jenkins**

Some of my modeling & acting bit parts are in:

Jo Jo Dancer
Hardball
Lucas

If you where like me, the struggle was very real in discovering my self-worth throughout my young adult years. Seen here, I was on a photo shoot pretending to be someone else like in the movie "Precious," because she was me. I was once sexually abused by my mother's boyfriend.

The shame and guilt of the act, definitely leaves a person in a nasty head space, but hearing that **"Jesus Loves You and God does too,"** were words that I just couldn't shake in those very ugly moments of my life. (*This photo was around the time I had a bit part in the Movie called Lady Blue*).

WHO AM I, WHO IS GOD!

So now, how does a girl go from looking like a floozy in this photo to becoming a minster, hosting a daily prayer line and more. *(Seen here in this photo, I was at the Taste Disco night club. I was looking for my boyfriend who was about to marry someone else. That smile covered up so much of pain).*

I was also that girl who was very distraught and disillusioned in my younger years. Not knowing much about **who I was** and where this life was leading me, but I'm thankful to God that my dance teacher (*Jewel McLaurin*) got a hold of me at an early age and wouldn't let go. She pushed me to become a professional dancer at Malcolm X College while pouring seeds of faith into my spirit as I began to recognize God's actions taking place in my life. In fact, God cared enough to send her and many others to watch over my soul before I knew it was happening.

> **God is what People finds that is divine in themselves. God is the best way we can behave in the ordinary occasions of life, and the farthest point to which we can stretch ourselves.**
> **By Max Lerner**

I can talk passionately about my past now, because it brought me to where I am today. **I received my License to preach, backed up with a Doctorate in Practical Counseling, a Bachelor's in Arts on Theological Communications and a Associates of Arts Degree in Liberal Arts** and it's all because I got a taste of God's divine presence. It was after he got my attention by any means necessary, especially with the career that I wanted the most. He also knew that I needed him the most.

(Seen here in the photo is our over 15 year plus Early Prayer line of which my sister (Minister Andrena Griffin and I started back in 2010).

Who is God? According to google, he's the supreme or ultimate reality: such as the being of perfection in power, wisdom and goodness who is worshipped as creator and ruler of the universe, and according to **(Psalms 36:5 - God's righteousness is immovable**, in other words, his standards are non-negotiable). It was his presence that made me whole. **I AM WHO, HE MADE ME TO BE!** Without his presence, I don't know where I would be.

WHAT IS PRAYER?

It took some serious understanding, valuable lessons, training and mentoring to get to my ministry destination. Like anything else, the school of hard knocks with life's experiences will show you the necessity of believing in something higher than your own ability, money, power, and connections.

Since, I thought that being a movie star would have been my ultimate prize, as it turns out, God was winning me through my pursuit of being a star which was the real prize. Although, this book is just 45 pages, I had to shorten the stories to get to the main points of my salvation. (*In this photo, I'd just turned 50 and still modeling. My first professional modeling job was in my twenties with Revlon, a major cosmetics company and lots more*).

> # Prayer may not always change things for you, but it for sure changes you for things.
> ## By Samuel M. Shoemaker

News Article by Carl West of Chicago

(*Seen here is a news clipping of my New 50 initiative. I didn't know that my photos after 50 would strike up such a conversation from other middle-age women, so much so, that I wanted to do more than just look pretty*). I was beginning to see more to my make up, than wearing make-up because of prayer.

It was when I began to talk to God, that I saw a woman of substance (*now valuing my self-worth*) staring back at me, after looking in the same old mirror for years, I'd began to change through prayer thus creating the leadership ability that others wanted to see.

What is Prayer? Communicating with God. According to the bible, (**James 5:16 — The prayer of a righteous man is powerful and effective and that the eyes of the Lord are on the righteous and his ears are attentive to their prayers**).

FAITH AND WORKS

How could I be considered righteous, when I'm still dressing like this. *Some would say that I'm being way too seductive to be saved (Seen here are photos that I posted on social media for my 50th birthday photo shoot which got me a lot of likes by the way, lol)* but, it just didn't sit right in my spirit.

I could simply say that modeling is what I do, but it's not my who! *(I'm doing it to make a living, but looking like, I'm being loose is not who I am).* I can also add that you have some professional actors like the **late Della Reese who was a ordained minister but yet, she was cursing up a storm in the Harlem Nights movie with Eddie Murphy and Red Foxx. Yeah, but this excuse doesn't work well for representing God.**

> # We cannot hand our faith to one another... Even in the Middle Ages, when faith was theoretically uniform, it was always practically individual. By John Jay Chapman

In case you don't know, once you become saved or walk in the will of God, there is a certain lifestyle, we should live by. It's called Holiness which also means watching what you wear and more. The bible tells us to dress in modest apparel which is definitely more acceptable than what I was wearing above, if I am to display holiness.

Since, I had a record of getting paid for wearing certain clothes which is what I considered work, I thought it was ok, and because I had faith in God to get those jobs.

Here's a scripture back up my claim; (**James 2:14, You have faith, and I have works, Show me your faith with out your works and I will show you my faith by works).**

KEYS TO SPIRITUAL SUCCESS →

*Faith
*Praise
*Prayer
*Fasting
*Worship
*Forgiveness
*Living Holy
*Go To Church
*Living Holy
*Sanctification
*Reading and
*Studying the
Bible

The one thing about God, is that he has a way of letting us know when we are wrong. There is a conviction that will nudge your spirit for correction. Was it more important to dress for a certain image to satisfy the world's standard of beauty or do I now dress to uphold God's standard of living, and why is it important to do so? In this analogy, the same rings true for keeping your space in God's good graces. Often, we have to choose our daily actions that coincides with God's will or will we not care and live sinfully and carelessly, thus causing many defeats from worldly troubles. To the right, are keys for spiritual success in victorious living. **It also includes igniting our will to even dress modestly**. *(1 Peter 3:3-4)*

> # Prayer crowns God with the honor and glory due to his name, and God crowns prayer with assurance and comfort. The most praying souls are the most assured souls.
> ## By Thomas B. Brooks

Now more subtle dress attire

After learning over the years and doing my best to be true to God's ways, there lies certain keys to spiritual success that will help you WIN along with God's help. *(You also need to realize that you are becoming an example of God's ways on the earth and you now have the ability to lead people somewhere based on what they see you do).* Do you want them to live victoriously or live in defeat? It's not cool to have to now pray for people, and to help them get delivered (free from the bondage of sin), after you have led them down that wrong path based on your actions *(It's called being hypocritical).*

Yes, posing to create a lustful image got me money, but being obedient to God's way got me money and so much more, prosperity, a peace of mind, a righteous name and God's trust in me as I can freely be led by his Holy Spirit.

WHAT DOES IT MEANS TO BE SAVED (OBTAINING SALVATION)?

(*Here is where I must warn you, YOU DO NOT HAVE WHAT IT TAKES TO STAY SAVED. YOU NEED JESUS TO HELP YOU ALONG THE WAY*). You must also know that **God's presence is known as the Holy trinity**, being one in the same person: He's our heavenly Father, the Son, Jesus Christ and the Holy Spirit, and they are all relevant in assisting us to obtain and sustain salvation (being saved). This process also goes along with using the list of keys from the previous page. Stay tuned as they will all be explained one by one.

First of all, lets talk about what it means to be saved, (*walking with God or having salvation and why is it so important*). **It means that you are giving up your old life to live a new life though Christ Jesus,** totally leaning on God's ways.

> ## The main lesson about prayer is just this: Do it! Do it! Do it! You want to be taught to pray? My answer is: pray.
> ## By John Laidlaw

The only way to have direct access to God is to acknowledge him personally with saying it publicly *(optional)* so that you can hear yourself affirm it to yourself, having your own clarity, out of your own mouth to God's ears. **"THAT YOU EXCEPT JESUS CHRIST AS YOUR LORD AND PERSONAL SAVIOR, ALSO STATING THAT YOU HAVE BEEN SEPARATED FROM HIM, REPENT FOR YOUR SINS, HAVING TURNED FROM YOUR WICKED WAYS TO BECOME BORN AGAIN IN CHRIST JESUS! (ROMANS 10:9)**

That wasn't too hard was it but, you also have to mean it in your heart. When it becomes a heart matter, you are making yourself vulnerable to letting the spirit of God come in, to change you for the better. Never think that you have to be perfect to experience God's love. It's very important to know this, so that you can often remind yourself of the vow

Delece is being honored at the Universoul Circus

you took while making the decision to chose God's ways in your daily living, in a world of so much uncertainty. How will your spirit arise to the occasion now, when you are under life's pitfalls, pressures and cares of this world?

PRAISE AND WORSHIP

That personal vow you made from the previous page, is also a profession of your **faith**. (Meaning that you must have a slight measure of belief in knowing that God will make life better for you as well). So now, how will you rise to occasion, will you fully activate your faith in God to handle your struggles? Will you go back to your old ways of not trusting him, or will you let him fix all of your problems and, you too. Remember, according to the bible after confessing the vow, you'll become a new creature in Christ, and should be ready to live for God. **(John 3:3) NO ONE CAN ENTER THE KINGDOM OF GOD UNLESS HE IS BORN OF THE SPIRIT).**

Delece worked on the movie **Lady Blue**

Let me go back to describing why these keys *(from page 10)* are very important if you want to stay in the vain of receiving God's guidance, favor, blessings and covering over your life.

> **Sometimes we think we are too busy to pray. That is a great mistake, for praying is a saving of time.**
> **By Charles Haddon Spurgeon**

Let's start with that word called **FAITH** *which is the substance or assurance of things we hope for, but have not yet received them— you can find another meaning in the bible,* **(Hebrews 11 — it's having confidence in what we hope for and assurance in what we do not see)** and **(Matthew 17:20 tells you that you only need faith as a size of a grain of a mustard seed).** Faith is the one word that you can not please God without.

Next on the list of keys to seeking spiritual success is **PRAISE.** I'll throw in **WORSHIP** here too, because they are somewhat similar. **(Psalms 22:3 tells us that God inhabits the Praises of his People).** If you want to pull God 's presence close to you in an instant, start giving him praise where ever you are. Did you know that you can change a somber atmosphere in any room when you praise God. You are inviting God's presence to be with you anywhere.

GOING TO CHURCH TO HELP WITH SPIRITUAL AWARENESS AND MORE

You can quickly enlighten a person's mood through the power of praise. The power of praise alerts God's spirit within us. Why do you think, that there are Choirs in churches. Before the preacher preaches, the choir commands praises to be ushered in with audience participation so that the atmosphere for God's invisible presence can easily be received by everyone. His invisible presence easily comes in when the Pastor preaches God's word. (The Pastor is supposed to be influenced by God's Holy Spirit while preaching).

Delece worked with UNCF

GOING TO CHURCH is also on the list of keys for seeking spiritual success, because they are known to be spiritual hospitals. It's a place of refuge for the sick, down trodden and for you too. The church is the only place where you will assemble under one roof with like-minded people to partake in God's corporate anointing.

> # Don't try to reach God with your understanding; that is impossible. Reach him in love; that is possible.
> # By Carlo Carretto

Under God's anointing, sick people can come to get healed, you can find peace and most importantly, you are learning God's ways, not only by the preacher but by the way other people are expressing their love for God, as well.

Delece was in the Movie, Weird Science

WHAT DOES IT MEAN TO HAVE A SPIRITUAL AWARENESS? (**Ephesians 6:12**) It is discovering the connection to something bigger than ourselves. It typically involves a search for greater meaning in life. If you look at scary movies, I'm sure you've heard about evil spirits vs. God's holy spirit. To know and under-stand that there's a choice in the spirit realm, just know only one way will lead you to God's victorious living by the guidance of his Holy Spirit only (This is what it means to be born again).

Upon discussing praise on the previous page, the act of **WORSHIP** goes hand in hand. Praising God welcomes you to his presence, but Worship takes you behind the veil where God's holy spirit dwells (*You may receive the gift of speaking in tongues in Worship from God*). Its a deeper expression of reverence and adoration for God.

Ms.Mahagony

Prophets who represents the voice of God, can tell you something about your past, present and/or future byway of the holy spirit through this level of worship. Worship is also a great weapon against worrying. Instead of wondering how things are going to turn out, learn how to worship before you began to worry. You are showing God that you are going to trust him to make a way. When you worship, you are also able to hear God's voice clearer. What you worship is what's important too. This point leads me to the next Key, **FASTING**.

Faith doesn't wait until it understands; in that case it wouldn't be faith. by Vance Havner

Beauty Pageant Winner *What is Fasting? (To give up somethings like food and etc., for the purpose of seeking God's spiritual strength),* **Matthews 6:6-18**. In these photos, I won a beauty pageant called Ms. Mahogany. We came across an Egyptian Museum in Wadsworth Wisconsin. Since, we as African Americans have a rich history pertaining to the Egyptian Culture, my director Mary Swopes, thought that it would be a good idea to take pictures in their costumes for fun. When I showed some other people the photo, they were upset because some Egyptians worshipped other Gods. This moment caused me to understand that you can worship someone and/or something other than God, like in the Ten Commandments and in doing so, made them miss their blessings. Fasting is a way to make sure you stay in

LAST OF THE KEYS — READING AND STUDYING THE BIBLE, LIVING HOLY, SANCTIFICATION, FORGIVENESS

Delece Worked in Brewster's Place

alignment with the will of God, being ever so careful that you are not making other things and people more important than God in your life.

During your sacred time to commune with God byway of fasting, some people fast from watching television and from using their cell phones, just to **READ AND STUDY THE BIBLE** for a closer connection in relationship to God's holy power. Your participation is a personal sacrifice for God's demonstration to aide in casting out demonic spiritual forces as well, but that's a whole other topic. **(Matthew 17:21 -But this kind of demon does not go out except by prayer and fasting).** Reading your bible is also a demonstration of how God operates through mankind concerning his connection which is powered by his Holy Spirit. Another name is **(Holy Ghost).**

(John 14:26 — But the Comforter, which is the Holy Ghost, whom the Father will send in my name, he shall teach you all things, and bring all things to your remembrance).

> # I have been driven many times to my knees by the overwhelming conviction that I had nowhere else to go. My own wisdom and that of all about me seemed insufficient for the day.
> ## By Abraham Lincoln

The last key to discuss is **FORGIVENESS.** I know that it is a difficult word to expand on, especially if someone really, I mean reaaally harmed you in some way, lied on you, back stabbed you and/or if you find out that you have frienemies. Forgiveness is more for you to free yourself from the control that person has over you in the matter. Learn to release and let it go

Kidz Korna Tv Show

in Jesus's name. I 'll tell you a important spiritual part about forgiveness, if you don't learn to forgive, your father in heaven may not forgive you and/or your ungodly ways. Remember, our goal is to be in right standing with God, and let

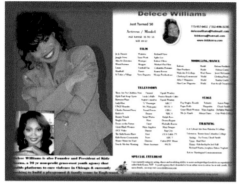

This acting/modeling composite was my ticket to salvation while pursuing show business and ended up on life's grand stage with GOD.

GOD'S GUIDANCE

God take care of your enemies. I didn't know that I was standing on the shoulders of Angels until I ended up in New York for the first time in my life with only thirty dollars in my pocket. I went to work for Producer, Director **SPIKE LEE**.

This trip was definitely a faith walk which stemmed from a pastor friend of mine. With his help, I was, all of a sudden on the set of JUNGLE FEVER, working with *Halle Berry, Ossie and Ruby Davis, Isaiah Washington, Wesley Snipes, Queen Latifah and Samuel L. Jackson*, some of the heaviest names in show business. My pastor friend felt that I was ready to handle this journey, since he knew that God was backing me up.

> # When a man takes one step toward God, God takes more steps toward that man than there are sands in the worlds of time.
> ## By The Work of the Chariot

In fact, the Pastor gave me the thirty dollars and paid for my plane ticket to go. I guess God allowed this opportunity for me because he also knew that he had to get my attention some kind of way. **(GOD HAS TAILOR MADE SITUATIONS CARVED OUT FOR YOU TOO, SO THAT HE CAN DEMONSTRATE HIS POWER IN YOUR LIFE. THIS IS WHY, YOU CAN'T LET NOT GROWING UP IN CHURCH BE YOUR EXCUSE FOR NOT SERVING GOD).**

Another one of Delece's Acting Headshots

I got many faith filled stories to talk about through my show business journey, but this moment was one of my biggest mind blowing ways that God revealed himself and his power to me directly. Before I go any further with the Spike Lee story, I didn't know about the keys of spiritual success at that time. What, I know is that I've been on several faith walk journeys, only for God to show up and show out for his glory and miraculous power to be revealed as an example to others.

THE FOOLISH THINGS

Getting back to the Spike Lee's story, because I was so scared and excited at the same time, I took my bible with me everywhere we where on the set of Jungle Fever. I was a fairly new believer at this time, but I wanted to show God that I was trying to be faithful to my salvation by not sleeping around and etc.

Delece's Modeling Photo Shoot.

Here is where my spiritual discernment (*having the knowledge of something*) really begin to kick in and I can surely tell you that those keys (from page 10) really works. Remember, I didn't grow up in church, but because God loved me so, as he loves all of us, he strongly got my attention through something that I wanted very badly. It was demonstrated in some of the strangest ways in my life, especially in this New York moment. (**He has chosen the foolish things of the world to confound the wise — 1Corinthians 1:27**) .

> **By learning to contact, listen to, and act on our intuition, we can directly connect to the higher power of the universe and allow it to become our guiding force.**
> **By Shakti Gawain**

Spike himself laughed at me and thought I was strange because I would not leave my bible behind. To make a long story short, while I was sleeping one night in Spike's sister apartment while using my bible as a pillow, a vision of the sky opened up. Words from a bible scripture (**Isaiah 55:11**) came flashing across my room ceiling. (**It stated that God's ways are not our ways, nor is his thoughts, our thoughts and that God's words does not return unto him void**). This is why I can quote this scripture any time and anywhere. I didn't have to really wake up out of this dream (vision), because I was half sleep when I was shown the scripture. God definitely let me know that he was with me in New York and that he had plans for my life. This experience awakens in my thought process every time, I would have doubt or get discouraged regarding God's promises for my life. It's a reminder that God will eventually, show up and show out for me.

Delece at the White House

ANGELS ARE REAL

More Modeling Photos

One time back in Chicago, I was trying to get to class but couldn't. Money was not plentiful as always for an struggling college student. I was living upstairs in my grandmother's apartment building with my 5 year old daughter.

Gut wrenching tears fell, due to the disappointment of being in constant financial struggles even though I was trying to better my situation. Those tears must have reached heaven in that moment, because while I was standing there trying to figure out what to do, a five dollar bill fell on my bed. No one else was in the room, at least we thought. My daughter witnessed it too. She picked it up because it fell right next to her.

> # God is to me that creative force, behind and in the universe, who manifests himself as energy, as life, as order, as beauty, as thought, as conscience, as love.
> # By Henry Sloane Coffin

God has done it again! It was later revealed to me that it was an angel in my room who placed it there. I have had at least five angelic experiences that I can vividly recall. Another time, my daughter and I was in the Evergreen Plaza Shopping Center. We were looking at cards in the Hallmark Store which only had four small aisles. This strange looking woman came down the center aisle as if she was floating through the place. She ended up directly in front of me with piercing pearl looking eyes, with drawn on eye brows and a wig. She was

wearing a overcoat and smelled so loudly with a flamboyant cold scent coming from the bed of flowers, like in the Color Purple movie. She rubbed my heart and said "do not be afraid, I had a little drink this morning." (*She was referring to a drink from God's living water, the rivers of life*).

She asked me to choose between two cards that she had in her hands which was talking about 50th anniversaries. I quickly and nervously pointed to the first card. Then she said ok, turned around and walked away, but I never seen her leave the store. It was as if she disappeared in the next aisle, but again in that moment, my daughter found a five dollar bill in her pocket, and I didn't put it there. Later that day, my grandparents were announcing that they had been married for 50 years.   Immediately, it hit me. God wanted me to honor my Grandparents. I was blessed to put together there anniversary with the favor of God. I didn't have to pay for things needed and I got a limousine driver to pick them up for free. They were so happy and it wasn't too much longer before they went home to be with the lord at separate times.

> # Your mind cannot possibly understand God, your heart already knows. Minds were designed for carrying out the orders of the heart.   By Emmanuel

Now that I think about it, God's Favor has been better than money, even though we need money but more importantly, we need Gods favor, grace and mercy even more. We are not always right, but as I have shown him my willingness to desire him more than anything and he has consistently shown me his mighty hand through his holy ghost power, through angelic beings, through preachers and my special ministry friend *Apostle Ola Wilson.*

She labored with me on so many personal levels so that I could closely learn the ways of God. God didn't stop there.   He has also given me my heart's desires (**Psalms 37:4 — If you walk up right, I'll give you your heart's desires**) from some careers goals to marrying the man of my dreams, *Farley Williams whose famously known as Farley Jackmaster Funk, the King of House Music* to having children, along with now being a grandma. So, how do I give up on God's ways now, just to **STRADDLE THE FENCE?**

Delece and her husband at church Praising God.

MY MANY BLESSINGS

I was blessed to work several times with *Oprah Winfrey, Richard Pryor, Keanu Reeves, Kenya Moore, be mentored by Alex Haley* and so many more. God speared my life the night *Notorious Big, the famous Rapper* was murdered, Thank You Jesus! I only experienced one minor casting coach situation with the late great *Ron O'neal (the man who starred as Super-fly in the 70's)*. Lord, thank you for spearing me whenever I went to these different cities to explore acting/modeling opportunities. Lord you even allowed me to meet many of my favorite inspirational singers; the great *Shirley Ceasar, Yulonda Adams, Tramaine Hawkins, Albertina Walker, Pops Staples, Tye Tribbett, Mary, Mary* and more in which their songs carried me through many dark hours.

> **All who call on God in true faith, earnestly from the heart, will certainly be heard, and will receive what they have asked and desired.**
> **By Martin Luther**

God even shielded me from the situation that I had with **R. Kelly**. Some may know that I too was one of his hair braiders, but there was also much more to this story which will be told another book, so stay tuned.

One particular scripture that I need to discuss now is (**Matthew 6:24, No one can serve two masters. Either he will hate the one and love the other. We can't serve both God and mammon (biblical term for riches)**. God is constantly warning us that he will only do things his way, so that he can reign supreme in our lives. So, how do you now balance the two, especially since we live in this world. We work in this world and live around people that do not know God's ways which can also cause us to be in between trying to please them and God at the same time.

Modeling After 50

> # The person who has a firm trust in the Supreme Being is powerful in his power, wise by his wisdom, happy by his happiness.
> ## By Joseph Addison

Straddling the fence is a refence point to what some elders may say when they feel like, we got one foot in the world and the other foot in the church, (*and that you will only pick God's way up when you need him to get you out of trouble, but won't completely dedicate your life to him*). In this case, you'll be torn between the influences of this world, that will and can cause you to put God's way on the back burner. **(Romans 8:35-39 tells us to let nothing separate you from the love of God).** Given my history and how God has dealt with me

and especially since I still work in my very interesting profession. I have now learned how TO BE THE FENCE, (*the foundation that helps someone else get over to the Jesus's side. Another Christian word for it is to be an Evangelist).* Trust me, problems won't stop coming but, I'm too afraid to deal with them without God, which is what keeps me grounded in his ways.

In fact, the **next 20 pages** are work book ready. They are designed as a intimate guide for you to self-examine and reflect as a way of helping to determine how to get closer to God. Knowing God's ways and having a personal relationship is so important to daily victorious living in your personal and professional life.

Towards the end of the book, we have information for you to join our daily prayer line in case you need help with your answers. Learn how to pray for the salvation of your family members; loved ones and lots more..lets get started.

We are here to answer your questions, regarding your spiritual journey.

Our team of prayer warriors are always available to pray with you, but most importantly, our Lord and Savior Jesus Christ is always available to help you. <u>We have been praying daily for over 15 years now</u>, as we will continue command our days victorious, with you in mind (Job 38:12).

BEFORE YOU CLOSE THE BOOK, SEE WHO'S VERY PQWERFUL THAT NOTICED ME

News article by: CARL WEST

Beyond my wildest dreams, I never thought that I'd one day visit the **White House** and later become a certified agent, (given authority to bestow honor to others). *The current U.S. President in the highest office of the land signs the awards to honor deserving individuals whose committed to volunteer service.*

Upon me receiving that same honor, (**the Prestigious Presidential Lifetime Achievement Award),** to date, I've honored hundreds of exceptional individuals collectively cumulating over 500,000 volunteer service hours, and it's all because I decided to keep moving in spite of, to become the greatest version of me.

Upon discovering the fact that **doing is being,** it made me realize that after hanging around all of these stars, important people, dignitaries and etc., I may not be as powerful as some, but what I was doing, is being the best me that I can be and someone powerful noticed. **Thank you GOD!**

My
Other Projects

*US Honors Program

*CIF Ministry Productions

*Queens Awards Ceremony

uspresidentialsawards.com
queensrewarded.com

*Kidz Korna, NfP
www.kidzkorna.com

MY HELP COMES:

♦ Through *Communication* and the *Wisdom of Elders,*

♦ Having *Tunnel Vision* from the pain of my Ancestors to keep PUSHing (Pray Until Something Happens) through, and

♦ Lastly, from being in tuned with **GOD's** grace for *Spiritual Guidance, Instruction* and *Strength* to create my own lane for victorious living and you can have victorious living too.

For More info go to (www.drdelece.com).

Dr. Delece's Back Story for producing this book.

The goal was to help guide you through some battlefields of your life using words of wisdom. Did you know that there is POWER in what you say to yourself. In the Bible (Proverbs 18:21), it tells us that Life and Death is in the power of your tongue? What you say, makes a great deal of differences with your circumstances and just know that GOD WILL BACK YOU UP, if you allow it be so.

This **STAR STUDDED** Inspirational montage of quotes has wisdom notes for every *GENERATION AND MANY SITUATIONS* collaged on each page as I talked about my journey for success.

Dr. Delece Williams

I WENT BACK TO GO FORWARD

At around sixteenish, my siblings and I had a pet <u>CALF</u>.

Most girls grow up with a puppy, hamster, bird or even a garden snake for a pet. There I was sitting with a calf, not realizing the significance of this photo until now. Yes, it was definitely impossible at that time to understand it for sure.

It has also indulged me with memories of my sweet sixteenish years, recalling the excitement in life as I began searching for bigger and better adventures to aim for beyond family concerns, classmates connections and school activities.

Life was actually going to soon happen without living at home and I needed to figure out how to turn my dreams into reality, what direction to take, what moves to make or was I going to find all the answers by going to College.

In case you are thinking, why are you talking about a cow in this moment, glad you asked! That cow represented the <u>maturity</u> (**HAVING REACHED FULL DEVELOPMENT**) of which most 16 year olds definitely don't know much about. It usually comes as you get older, and that I surely needed it in my next phase of life.

No one knows a clear path of discovering yourself, your mission and/or your future while looking through the eyes of your youth, like the young me on the other page, to becoming the blossoming adult that I was aspiring to be on this page. Hindsight is definitely 20/20 and we most certainly don't have a measuring stick of solutions to help make goals obtainable unless you have experiences from others, our instincts, wit and knowledge to help you along the way.

I remember wearing this dress to the Naacp Image Awards in the early 90's during my reign as Ms. Mahogany, a beauty pageant winner. Upon meeting many celebrities backstage, my shoe heel broke. It was a gentleman from a fancy store in Hollywood California that gave me a pair of $300 dollar shoes for free and told me to always remember to help someone else along the way. He had also spoke into my spirit that led me to believe that I could be someone great one day.

It has always been words of wisdom that stuck with me while navigating my goals from working in television, producing, writing, to modeling and helping to shape young bright minds for **over 30** years, along with marrying a world famous Music Producer/DJ and friend of over **38 years**. Words of wisdom has always help to sharpen my intuition, giving me light at the end of the tunnel thus creating a pathway for my ends to meet. Thanks God for victorious living today and the strength to help others along the way. Hope this was helpful!

Work as if you
were to
live one hundred years:
Pray as
if you were
to die tomorrow.

By Benjiman Frankin

Thanks for supporting
"ON THE SHOULDERS OF ANGELS,"

MORE OF DR. DELECE'S BOOKS

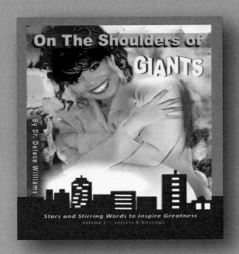

ON THE SHOULDERS OF GIANTS
Volume 1 - Lessons & Blessings

ON THE SHOULDERS OF GIANTS
Volume 2 - Advice For Young People
Youth Edition

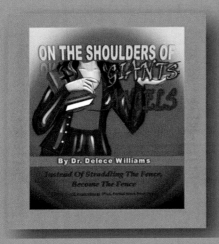

ON THE SHOULDERS OF ANGELS
All Inspirational
Includes Partial Workbook Pages

IT'S SOMETHING ABOUT GRANDMAS
Co-Authors, Dior and Dion
Delece's Grandchildren

BE ON THE LOOK OUT FOR :
"IN THE HOUSE WITH A KING,"

A Book on Marriage & Relationships

FOR MORE DETAILS, GO TO:
WWW.DRDELECE.COM

TAKE THIS WITH YOU, IN CASE YOU NEED IT

Here are a few more biblical scriptures to help you get to some quick solutions upon learning to spend some quality time God's word.

IN THE BIBLE, YOU CAN GO HERE FOR

SUPPORT...........................ROMANS 5:5

WISDOM.............................JAMES 1:15

PURPOSE..........................ROMANS 8:28

BLESSINGS................. EPHESIANS 1:3-4

INSPIRATION................2 TIMOTHY 3:16

GUIDANCE.......................PROVERBS 1:5

VICTORY................................1 JOHN 5:4

UNDERSTANDING........PROVERBS 16:22

WORRY..........................PHILIPPIANS 4:6

CHANGE......................PHILIPPIANS 3:21

HOPE..................................ROMANS 5:5

PRAYER.........................PROVERBS 15:29

FORGIVENESS...............MATTHEWS 6:14

PRAYER.........................PROVERBS 15:29

FORGIVENESS.............. MATTHEWS 6:14

RESPECT.......1 THESSALONIANS 5:12-13

SELF-REFLECTION

WORKBOOK

PAGES

PUTTING GOD FIRST

HOW TO FIND AND REACH GOD
When we lose God, it is not God who is lost.
By Anon

The best way to strengthen your relationship with God is to PUT HIM FIRST. Spending quality time and staying connected to his ways, carries you into a deeper relationship with God's purpose in your life. The next several pages can assist you with this journey as you write down your thoughts upon engaging these scriptures.

PUTTING GOD FIRST (*EXODUS 20:3 — Thou shall have no other Gods before me*). What do you need to do in order to put him first?

_____

_____

_____

_____

_____

_____

_____

_____

_____

_____

_____

_____

_____

_____

_____

_____

_____

_____

_____

_____

_____

ATTITUDE

(PHILIPPIANS 2:5– *You must have the same attitude that Christ Jesus had***)**. What attitude will you have, and do think Jesus would be pleased with how you are approaching this exercise?

_____
_____
_____
_____
_____
_____
_____
_____
_____
_____
_____
_____
_____
_____
_____
_____
_____
_____
_____
_____
_____
_____
_____
_____
_____
_____
_____
_____

ASKING GOD FOR HELP

(MATTHEW 7:7-8– *Ask, and it shall be given to you; seek, and you shall find; knock, and it shall be opened to you. For everyone who asks receives, and he who seeks finds, and to him who knocks, it will be opened*). What's your ask?

_____
_____
_____
_____
_____
_____
_____
_____
_____
_____
_____
_____
_____
_____
_____
_____
_____
_____
_____
_____
_____
_____
_____
_____
_____
_____

ANXIETY

(1 PETER 5:7 – *Cast all your cares (anxieties) on him because he cares for you!).* Tell God about your problems right here?

_____

_____

_____

_____

_____

_____

_____

_____

_____

_____

_____

_____

_____

_____

_____

_____

_____

_____

_____

_____

_____

_____

_____

_____

_____

_____

_____

_____

_____

GOD'S GUIDANCE

(PROVERBS 3:5:6 – *Trust in the Lord with all thine heart, and lean not unto your own understanding; in all of your ways, acknowledge him and he will lead your path***).** This scripture definitely fits in times of indecisiveness, not clearly making right decisions also lingering in a state of confusion, write your analogy here if this is you or someone you know?

_____

_____

_____

_____

_____

_____

_____

_____

_____

_____

_____

_____

_____

_____

_____

_____

_____

_____

_____

_____

_____

_____

_____

_____

_____

_____

_____

GRATITUDE

(PROVERBS 10:6 — Blessings crowns the head of the right-eous). What are you grateful for, although you maybe facing some challenges?

_____

_____

_____

_____

_____

_____

_____

_____

_____

_____

_____

_____

_____

_____

_____

_____

_____

_____

_____

_____

_____

_____

_____

_____

_____

_____

_____

_____

_____

_____

LISTENING TO GOD

(ISAIAH 55:3– *Come to me with your ears wide open. Listen and find your life*).   To live a life, listening to God is the best way of life. Yes!...God does talk to us but the question is, are you in a position to listen and if so, how?

_____
_____
_____
_____
_____
_____
_____
_____
_____
_____
_____
_____
_____
_____
_____
_____
_____
_____
_____
_____
_____
_____
_____
_____
_____
_____
_____
_____
_____
_____
_____
_____

PATIENCE

"Patience is the companion to wisdom," by St Augustine
(PROVERBS 19:11 – A person's wisdom yields patience).
Once you feel that you have heard from God and acted accordingly (*in prayer, fasted, praise and etc*), your patience is everything in waiting to get God's results, are you patient in waiting on God to response?

_____
_____
_____
_____
_____
_____
_____
_____
_____
_____
_____
_____
_____
_____
_____
_____
_____
_____
_____
_____
_____
_____
_____
_____
_____
_____

DEALING WITH CHANGE

(ECCLESIASTES 3:1– *To everything there is a time and a season, and a time to every purpose under the heaven***).** Our world is in a constant state of change, but God is not. At some point we all must face change. Do you believe that the same God who created the universe, is the same God that can help you through life's changes?

_____
_____
_____
_____
_____
_____
_____
_____
_____
_____
_____
_____
_____
_____
_____
_____
_____
_____
_____
_____
_____
_____
_____
_____
_____
_____
_____

PRIORITIES

(MATTHEW 6:33– *Seek ye first the kingdom of God and all of his ways, then all of your needs will be met*). What's stopping you, did you know that you may be holding up your own blessing by not doing so. What do you need to change if you are not seeking him and putting him first?

_____

_____

_____

_____

_____

_____

_____

_____

_____

_____

_____

_____

_____

_____

_____

_____

_____

_____

_____

_____

_____

_____

_____

_____

_____

_____

PRESEVERANCE

(GALATIANS 6:9 – *Let us not become weary in doing good, for at the proper time, we will reap a harvest if we do not give up).* Everyone gets discouraged, are you going to give up or get up with God's help?

_____
_____
_____
_____
_____
_____
_____
_____
_____
_____
_____
_____
_____
_____
_____
_____
_____
_____
_____
_____
_____
_____
_____
_____
_____
_____
_____
_____
_____
_____

PROCRASTINATION

(JAMES 1:22 – *But prove yourselves doers of the word, and not merely hearers who delude themselves***). According to Ben Franklin, did you know that "One Day is Worth Two Tomorrows,"** Are you putting off 3 days worth of blessings by putting off prayer, how can you change it?

_____
_____
_____
_____
_____
_____
_____
_____
_____
_____
_____
_____
_____
_____
_____
_____
_____
_____
_____
_____
_____
_____
_____
_____
_____
_____

UNDERSTANDING

(PSALMS 119:33– *Teach me, O Lord, the way of your statues, and I shall keep it to the end***).** With all of your heart, are you asking God for his understanding and purpose concerning your daily actions and decision making?

_____
_____
_____
_____
_____
_____
_____
_____
_____
_____
_____
_____
_____
_____
_____
_____
_____
_____
_____
_____
_____
_____
_____
_____
_____
_____
_____
_____
_____
_____

RESPONSIBILITY

(GALATIANS 6, verses 4 & 5 – *But each person should examine his own work, in himself alone, and not in respect to someone else. For each person will have to carry his own load*). Who's responsible for your behavior? As a side note: God's word says that you are...if you obey God's ways, you will be blessed in countless ways, but if you ignore his teachings, you must eventually bear the consequences of those irresponsible decisions. Where does your responsibility lie in the matter of receiving your blessings?

_____
_____
_____
_____
_____
_____
_____
_____
_____
_____
_____
_____
_____
_____
_____
_____
_____
_____
_____
_____
_____
_____
_____

SPIRITUAL GROWTH

(2 Timothy 1:6 – *I remind you to fan into flames the spiritual gifts God gave you***).** Spiritual growth is always possible. God will help us become what we are meant to be for his glory. Every day is an opportunity to live, to love, to serve and to grow in God's ways….How are you daily growing spiritually?

_____

_____

_____

_____

_____

_____

_____

_____

_____

_____

_____

_____

_____

_____

_____

_____

_____

_____

_____

_____

_____

_____

_____

_____

_____

PRAYER

(PHILIPPIANS 4:6 – Be anxious for nothing, but in everything by prayer and supplication with thanksgiving, let your requests be made known to God). **Here's a quote by Corrie Ten Boom. Ask yourself; Is your prayer a steering wheel or a spear tire?**

_____
_____
_____
_____
_____
_____
_____
_____
_____
_____
_____
_____
_____
_____
_____
_____
_____
_____
_____
_____
_____
_____
_____
_____
_____
_____
_____
_____
_____
_____
_____
_____

NEGATIVITY

(PSALM 118:5 – *In my distress I prayed to the Lord, and he answered me and set me free*). Here's a quote by Max Lucado; God never promises to remove us from our struggles. He does promise, however, to change the way we look at them. Avoid arguments, but when a negative attitude is expressed, counter it with a positive and optimistic opinion. Are you developing a positive attitude by working continually to find what is uplifting and encouraging until your situation changes? If not, explain to yourself why not...

_____
_____
_____
_____
_____
_____
_____
_____
_____
_____
_____
_____
_____
_____
_____
_____
_____
_____
_____
_____
_____
_____
_____
_____

SELF-EXAMINATION

Now, are you getting to know your Godly spiritual self better? **(MATTHEW 7:3-5 –** *And why worry about a speck in your friend's eye when you have a log in your own eye? How can you think of saying to your friend, "Let me help you get rid of that speck in your eye," when you can't see the log in your own eye; then you will see well enough to deal with the speck in your friend's eye*). As you journey through life, you should continue to become better acquainted with yourself and have mercy on others for this reason. Can you now have compassion for others, knowing that we are not perfect as we try to be?

_____
_____
_____
_____
_____
_____
_____
_____
_____
_____
_____
_____
_____
_____
_____
_____
_____
_____
_____
_____
_____
_____
_____

Printed in the United States
by Baker & Taylor Publisher Services